FUN with "Fears & Phobias"

R U

In This Book?

Joey Edmonds

Author: of Joey Edmonds~ *Claustrophobic!*

FUN

with

"Fears & Phobias"

ISBN: 978-0-578-03701-1

www.JoeyEdmonds*Claustrophobic*.com
@Amazon.com

To the classiest, most honest and knowledgeable human I have ever met!

(Wife of 40 Years)

LYNN BILEK EDMONDS

Author of:

I ONLY HAVE TROUBLE WITH PEOPLE...
@Amazon.com

AUTHORS NOTES

Two years ago while preparing my first book, "JOEY EDMONDS ~ *Claustrophobic"* I set up a YOUTUBE site inviting others to tell me about their "Fears & Phobias". I received hundreds of stories, but was intrigued that no one volunteered their name! The realization that we who have these anxieties are not comfortable talking about them became the basis of my College & University 'FEARS & PHOBIAS' FUN ~ Seminar!

In the late 60's to the early 80's I was half of the unique Comedy Team EDMONDS & CURLEY, the first comedians to exclusively tour Colleges & Universities! (2,500) In addition, my amazing partner THOM CURLEY and I appeared on 50 TV talk shows, including

numerous times on the TONIGHT SHOW starring Johnny Carson! Here I am three decades later, hosting my seminar at our nations' colleges, often with son GRANT as part of our Grant & Joey "Love & Fear" Lecture Program.

The stories gathered during the writing of this book are all true…except for the ideas I created sometime during the middle of the night with the question What if? It might have happened! It could have happened! Create it! Someone must have had a similar anxiety!

Growing up in Wisconsin (Oshkosh) I was thrilled to be part of 5 seasons each year: Winter, Spring, Summer, Fall, & the Green Bay Packers! Aunt Arietta has had Packers' season tickets for over 50 years and in 1967 she & I huddled together in minus 36 degrees below zero weather during the Packers/Cowboys 'Ice Bowl Game', separating just long enough

to down another brandy! I always have had FUN and have tried anything and everything. Usually a ball was involved! (Often in this book I may invite you to imagine things…i.e. number of fun things to do with a ball. I could waste time spelling it out for you, but we both have better things to do!) I learned to tap dance, sing, play guitar & banjo, and even volunteered to play the company snare drum in the army (though I had never played a drum prior to the audition). Water skiing, snow skiing, model airplanes, flying lessons (real plane), ice skating (including crossing frozen lakes with hand sails) and juggling (did you think of that when I mentioned fun with a ball?) were just part of my ADHD carried out in real life! At the age of 30 I advanced to the National 2 level AYSO Soccer Referee (another ball…on your list?).

"Fears & Phobias"

Since the creation of my "Fears & Phobias" FUN-Seminar, I now ask each person I meet..."Do you have any fear or phobia?" (DYHAFOP)

And the usual answer is something like..." My friend/wife/brother / sister/mother/dad/buddy/girl friend/co-worker...suffers from...

(Get the pattern? The answers concern others!) Many inquire why I ask (DYHAFOP)? I respond.

JE- "A couple of years ago I wrote a book titled JOEY EDMONDS- *Claustrophobic*!

Now, I'm writing the follow up, FUN with "FEARS & PHOBIAS" and I'm searching for unusual fears or phobias."

"Once again I ask them, do <u>you</u> have any fear or phobia? <u>DYHAFOP</u>?"

Most of their responses deal with the more common anxieties, i.e. " I hate snakes, heights, spiders, etc., etc., etc., etc., etc., etc., or elevators (high on my *Claustrophobic* list!)".

<u>OCEANS</u>

One recent response to <u>(DYHAFOP)</u> from a college student was very intriguing! Silence... and then... "I really don't think I have a fear."

Another moment of silence and finally… "Oceans"! With a smile "OK… I guess I fear Oceans".

JE- …"and where do you live?"

"IOWA!" She was so proud!

AUDITIONING

I am sometimes chosen to audition for a TV commercial and I joyfully go because I have fun and once in a while I get the role and make money. At each audition I ask some of the actors if they have any fear or phobia. "DYHAFOP?" Not all actors want to talk to others prior to an audition.

Me, I could care less. (Maybe that's why I don't get more roles?) One actor, a native of Japan who spoke perfect English, said he had a fear of auditions until one time a director asked him to read the lines with an accent! The actor realized the director was 'suggesting' a Japanese accent… Instead, he used a perfect IRISH accent that had the director laughing on the floor! He said he never again had a Fear of auditioning.

Oh, and he got the role!

STAYING HOME
Agoraphobia

I was asked to be a 'judge' for a Comedy Contest this past year and prior to the competition, a guy in his forties with a cane approached me. He introduced himself and made my day by telling me how much he enjoyed my book JOEY EDMONDS ~*Claustrophobic*. We chatted and he informed me he suffered from Agoraphobia. I asked how that was working for him and he said for over a year he never left his house. Friends would help him with food, etc. and of course always offer to take him outside for a walk to the corner a hundred feet away.

After a year he convinced himself to take the walk by himself. The first ninety-eight feet were fine until he got to the corner and was greeted by a cyclist who upended the two of them.

I asked "What were your thoughts at that moment?" He replied that after telling the cyclist the situation, they both laid there and laughed! A few days later he had knee surgery and will have a constant partner with him for life… His Cane!

HEIGHTS

Sometimes with the assistance of a close friend or family member, a fear or phobia can be altered for someone with extreme anxiety. Before my seminars I have participants fill out an F & P Card (Fears & Phobias) with their birth date (no names are used) and their Fear or Phobia.

I then pick a card and ask June 1st if he or she would like tell their story. If there is silence I move on to another card. Just reading the fear or phobia of the June 1st card informs all in attendance of that anxiety. June 1st told us her story!
Last summer my friend convinced me to take a roller coaster ride at a theme park. I giggled nervously waiting in the line that only heightened my fear. Finally it was our turn and I insisted my friend get in first. That was not a good idea…the moment she got in I moved toward the exit. An attendant grasped my arm and turned me back to my seat. It was as if my friend had alerted the attendant. I am now in my seat with the safety bar over my chest waiting to ride!

[NOTE: *Claustrophobia* does not allow this author to ride a roller coaster…the safety bar over my chest is unbearable!]

After an excruciating length of time we started the long slow upward climb to 'somewhere'. I watched the ground slowly drop away, and clutched my friend. I was blabbering "I'll never go with you again"! and other nonsensical statements. We reached the top and started our descent and for the next 2 minutes I screamed non-stop! Finally the ride ended and the safety bar was released. I jumped out of my seat and to the amazement of us both, I turned to my friend and shouted, "Let's go again"! I wish I had a picture of her face! I will never forget her LOOK!

Later that summer I sky dived for the first time! I have no idea what came over me, but what a wonderful change in my life!

CLOWNS

Most children see a clown and their eyes light up. Some see clowns and turn away. There have been many clown stories thru the years created by 'grown ups'. Parents remember the angst toward their mom or dad for introducing them to a clown.

"Mommee Daddee why is that person dressed like that?"
M/D "Because he's a clown."
"How do you know it's a boy?"
M/D: "Well it could be a girl."
"When the clown gets close to us, will you ask?"
Why? Why? Why? Why?

This is one of those moments you can add your own dialog. It could go on for some time!)

One of the stories I cherish was a student who recalled her first childhood experience with a clown. For her 5th birthday her parents hired a female clown who wore the usual outfit with blond pigtails. The party was a success and the clown was a big hit! That night after she drifted off to dreamland, mom & dad placed a life size blow-up clown at the foot of her bed.

When she awoke to visit the potty, she was introduced to a plastic clown with blond pigtails that stared at her and did not move! <u>Now that is Fear!</u>

We wonder why we have so many screwed up kids! We have all seen the best clown delight a group of children; however, if even one child gets fearful, 'the horse is out of the barn'! Send the clown and everybody else home!

PUPPETS

I have known ventriloquist TAYLOR MASON for over 25 years. His show is second to none because of his many talents. His piano playing is superb and the songs he creates are suitable for an audience of any age.

Like all ventriloquists, Taylor has more than one puppet. My favorite was his 'SUMMO WRESTLER'. I say WAS because my agency years ago booked him in the college market and one performance was at a campus within a few miles of my home. Prior to the show I visited with him in his hotel suite, and after chatting awhile he soon made his way to the bathroom for a shower.

Sitting on a large chair was SUMMO! I picked up a magazine and leafed through some pages, all the time glancing at SUMMO staring at me. After a few moments I decided to alter the direction of SUMMO'S frozen gaze and turned his chair a few degrees in the opposite direction. Apparently I altered his center of gravity!

Out of the corner of my eye, SUMMO performed a slow silent forward tumble to the floor. ARRGG ...I screamed, just as Taylor entered from the bathroom! We both had a good laugh! I'm glad this event happened to me as an adult. A five year old would still be in therapy!

DOGS

When I was five I often played with a black and white dog from across the street. I don't know what happened, but the loveable black & white pooch on that day decided my right thumb was an appetizer! In addition to the pain, watching blood 'leaking' from my favorite hand created a memory I vividly recall. Even today I slowly drop my hand palm down and let a dog sniff my hand. If that tail stops wagging I'm out of there. For 19 years in Chicago our cat (Miss Kitty) would surprise me daily by leaping up on my desk. I'm ADHD…

…additional excitement I do not need!

FLYING ROUND OBJECTS

Thanks to TiVo, we never miss JEOPARDY! It is the best game show ever! I enjoy it not because I correctly answer 3 or 4 questions per show, but because my wife Lynn's breadth of knowledge is amazing. Each episode reveals places, things, and subjects I have never even heard of. Two or three times a year they have the teen-age contestants. ("How does he/she know that question?" is often one of my responses!)

Midway thru the JEOPARDY round, Alex chats with each contestant. Recently a young man 'coined' a new fear…let's call him Ethan! It seems he and dad were hitting golf balls in a large expansive field. After hitting a bag of balls, his dad walked to where the once hit golf balls lay (this is where I realized Ethan's 'smarts' came from mom) and proceeded to hit them back to his son. One of the Flying Round Objects hit his son on the top of his head. He did not lose consciousness, but sustained quite a bump. Fear of Flying Round Objects is now known as:

Areo Cranis Fear & Phobia!

DANCING

Anyone/Everyone/All of us/Young or old Male or Female etc, etc, etc! can all dance! Fear of dancing is actually two fold… Sashaying to the dance floor is #1, and #2 is what to do when one gets there. The first time a hand in hand middle school couple make their way to a dance floor, all anxieties built up during the week prior come to fruition. Game time has arrived! …giggles, the looks, the deep breathing, the friends, sweaty palms, the nerves…then everything unnatural comes together!

I was fortunate to have taken ballroom as well as tap dancing lessons at an early age (10-12) in the early 50's. In nursing school (yes, I have a nursing degree…no longer valid) I was assigned to help 13 year old Melissa, a newly diagnosed diabetic. I taught her to inject insulin with a syringe. (I gave myself a saline solution 'shot' assuming it would have a positive effect on her…it did!) The next day I jokingly asked, "What would you like to learn today"? We chatted for a while and I assumed there was nothing else. After a moment of silence…she looked at me and asked, "Do you know how to dance?" Long story short, the following week was to be the first middle school dance and she had never danced.

I stood in front of her with my arms extended, hands on her shoulders and she reached up and did the same.

We spent 20 minutes 'waltzing' and then it was time for her insulin. The next day she went home and I never saw her again. A week later when I reported to the nurses' station, there was an envelope for NURSE JOEY! Inside was a white piece of paper with two stick figures dancing! And at the bottom,

"Thank You"

GROWING OLD

The first time I hosted my "Fears & Phobias FUN-Seminar" at a college, I moved to the portion in the seminar where I read the F & P cards.

"January 23rd....Growing Old. Would you like to elaborate?" A beautiful model-type lady stood up and I asked her age (she was 18). I wondered why at 18 she was concerned about growing old. She said it had nothing to do with dying... she was not afraid to die. She observed how too many times young people mistreat senior citizens.

Being rude, dismissive, and the worst, ignoring them. She continued by revealing to us that her summer job was working part time in a nursing home. I wish I had taped that discussion. It continued for 20 minutes with many others joining in. At the end of the seminar I reminded them that I am slowly growing older and if perchance we should meet again, do not IGNORE ME!

DARKNESS

The following is my compilation of thoughts about *DARKNESS*! …my feelings… my ideas…nothing to do with medical fact, it is just JOEY logic! Ready? Okay.

When I entered this world I left behind a small, safe home, the only home I ever had… a home that had only *darkness*. Suddenly I'm thrust into light…blinding light…my 2nd trauma! (1st being the canal I struggled to leave behind.) Now if I can only rid myself of this searing light. It hurts so much I am making loud noises. I've never done this before! When I make this noise I return to darkness! Something is strange here… When I make the noise my eyes close and when I stop the noise I see light. This is going to be interesting. Soon the light seemed to soften and my noises ceased. I don't recall what happened next, but what a hoot that was! Like all of us, I eventually discovered I have a lot of space in which to maneuver. Lay on my back…roll to the left I'm on my stomach.

What fun! Oh oh, my eyes are open, but it is still dark! What the...?
I surmised there were things I didn't know. I started walking when I was 8 months old. This meant that when I left the bed I could walk around my room in the dark and bump into objects I could not see. I stubbed my toes… banged my head on the door knob… tripped over a toy.

During daylight hours I studied the location of objects and the door knob. Serious observations I have continued my entire life. Traveling to 2,500 colleges & universities with partner Thom Curley meant a different motel each night. I always slept with the bathroom light on! *DARKNESS*! Fear of the *UNKNOWN!*

AIR TRAVEL

Some of you have absolutely no fear of flying! You are so lucky! I wrote my book JOEY EDMONDS ~ *Claustrophobic* because one of the major airlines changed equipment (2 seats-aisle-2 seats) instead of (3 seats-aisle-3 seats) SURPRISE! I was not psychologically prepared to board that aircraft and when the flight attendant informed me she was about to close the hatch, I grabbed my suitcase and went home. The next day I flew a similar smaller aircraft and had no problems. What caused me to 'freak'?

(Adjust how you are sitting and follow along.) I always, always sit in an aisle seat and as far forward as possible. On one airline that does not assign seats, I'm a pre-board. When I ask the attendant for a pre-board they ask why and I tell them I'm *Claustrophobic.* The few times I have been challenged I give him/her my book and then conversations start…"my daughter is *Claustrophobic*, etc." I've actually sold books to flight attendants. I always board last or near the end of the line so I am not enclosed. Once I arrive at my assigned row it is a relief to find my seat has not been assigned twice. I have offered $20 a few times to avoid a middle or window seat. Most fellow passengers understand when I tell them I'm claustrophobic.

Twice I was forced into a window seat and 3 times middle seats. In those situations I order Bloody Marys! Once airborne I have no problems. Others have varied problems with air travel. I have learned to watch travelers disguise their fears in numerous ways. When boarding ~ when forcing 'stuff' into the overhead ~ closing the window blind ~ immediately trying to sleep. Numerous reactions during take off and landing ~ clasping hands in prayer fashion, mandatory closing of eyes and if you have a friend, holding their hand.

Occasionally applause on landing!

Were we meant to fly?

THUNDER & LIGHTNING

The Scene: Two 3 bedroom cabins- Main House – Dining room – Bar – Game Room – and six more bedrooms - Red Barn filled with hay across the street from the Dude Ranch-10 horses in the field next to the Red Barn! Huge Tree dwarfing the pool and Main House. Six Autos parked in the proximity of the Cabins. The Edmonds & 3 other families were playing volleyball. This was late July in Wisconsin and the temperature had been in the high 90's all week.

The sun was slowly sliding over the horizon when suddenly the sky turned ghoulishly black. Out of nowhere serious wind and rain appeared. I had been on the fringe of two previous tornados and I just knew this was number 3! Everyone ran to the Main House and within minutes all electricity vanished. Some of us ventured to the large porch that had no windows. Canvas covered the expansive length of the porch while the ends of each side were uncovered. The direction of the wind and rain was coming from one of the ends which we avoided. The other uncovered end provided quite a view of the barn across the street.

The horses sequestered themselves next to the barn while lightning provided a visual slide-show of the horses in panic mode, rearing up & down! It was scary and gorgeous at the same time. AND THEN… it went away as quickly as it had started. Electricity returned and we all gathered in the game room/bar area. Being someone always searching for fun I exclaimed: "Who wants to join me in the pool?" Lynn gave me the 'you will grow up soon look' and we all retired for the evening. Just another adventure at the

<u>T N T Dude Ranch</u>

MOTOR CYCLES

Each year on a Sunday in October, thousands of cycles and their owners participate in the LOVE RIDE, a charity event thru the Los Angeles/Burbank area. It is amazing to view neighbors riding their 'hogs' and waving to the thousands of pedestrians lining the route. Even Jay Leno joins in the fun. I'm guessing there are still clubs that may have friction with other clubs, but on that special day they are united for a wonderful civic cause.

Each weekend I watch an increasing number of couples dressed in biking apparel join other couples for rides to the numerous mountains for all day outings. To them and all bikers I say "Enjoy, but I will not be joining you."

Many years ago, three male nursing students (Jerry, Al, Joey) and our girl friends traveled to Al's farm in northern Wisconsin (Bloomer) for a weekend. All good memories except for one! Al's neighbor Tex owned the biggest motor-cycle I had ever seen. A Harley-Davidson with one huge seat that could house a family of five! Tex asked if anyone would like a ride. The other two couples declined. Lucy and I said sure!

Tex mounted the bike as if it were a Clydesdale horse. Lucy sat closely behind Tex and I behind both, clutching Lucy. The engine roared…Tex looked back and said "HANG ON"! He adjusted his 'Harley Hat' and off we went. Visualize five miles of straight country road. I knew we were going fast as I strained to peek at the speedometer over the shoulders in front me and saw 100 miles an hour. At that moment, Tex once again adjusted his hat with BOTH HANDS!

<u>NO HANDS on the bar!</u>

NEVER AGAIN!

LIFTING WEIGHTS

Except for 5 lb. hand weights, I have never "worked with weights" (is that the correct terminology?) Son Grant has continued with the weights he started in high school and has grown from 140 lbs. - 175 lbs.- all muscle. Daughter Kate has her own version of weights. A six pack of 12 oz. snap top cans! In our townhouse complex I made a new friend a few years ago who is a couple of years my junior and is a real outdoors man…hunting, fishing, target shooting and has the trophies to prove it. Let's call him…..Jim.

He also knows how to build or repair just about anything. We have nothing in common except our wicked senses of humor! He is also an every-other-day push-ups, small weights, big weights exercise guy! All the equipment set up in his garage. J. P. is another resident half our age and works in tandem with Jim. ...I spot you...you spot me. The three of us have fun. Mostly me watching them grunt & groan. One day on a trek to the grocery store I visited Jim's garage and after 'What's up dude' and a couple of silly comments, he said "You should have been here yesterday!" "Why?" I asked... "You could have spotted me." I was tempted to make one of my wicked retorts, but his tone was serious.

"What happened?" He then told me the first time he lifted the 238 lbs. bar everything was fine. After relaxing and following all the techniques lifters do, he went for another 238 lb lift. He got it up enough to clear, but could not raise it. The bar was now resting on his chest. He said he was thinking about calling out for some help, but he, being the macho dude he is, gave it another try. No luck. He then knew it was time to roll the bar downward. After getting the bar past his metal belt buckle, he was home free! I asked him if his wife knew and he made me promise "Not a word"!

Hope she enjoys this chapter!

SINGING

Singing falls into the FEAR category of dancing, speaking, and numerous individual sports. All these activities can be done in private (an excellent way to learn), but are extremely nerve racking until the 1,000th time! My DNA has been very good to me especially in the area of song.

My first solo was in 5th grade at St. Peter's school when a visiting nun spent the morning in our class indoctrinating the 24 of us in the many areas of 'catholic need to know.' Apparently she intended to teach us a song titled 'Lady of Fatima', that is until I joined in after one line creating an acappella duet and near the end I took over and finished solo.

The applause she started was a first and remains high in my memory bank! That afternoon class session was quite an ego builder. Our regular nun talked about what we shared in the morning and later asked if I would like to reprise 'Lady of Fatima'? Not as much applause this time. I learned it is always more fun singing with a partner!

I hated being part of the congregation during church services because you never knew the singing limitations of your pew mate! I silently applauded when others 'mimed' their singing although it really did look...what's the word......Stupid! If there was a choir I sang with the choir. There are members of my extended family who are not gifted with song. Mom and one or more of her sisters...!

Dad was just the opposite. He used to be the band singer in addition to playing saxophone in an orchestra. In 1974 Harry Chapin wrote a song titled MR. TANNER about a man with a magnificent voice who ran a dry cleaning plant but never allowed others to hear him sing. That was my father Edmund…the last 30 years he worked at home in the basement and was always singing until someone else entered his domain. Singing was personal to him. I think my dear daughter got that from Grandpa Putzer.

On the other hand, Grandpa Bilek never stopped singing (except during business hours at the bank). He was the life of every party. Everyone loved Frank!

Then there are those whose exuberance in the art of song is so infectious we could care less about the notes they fail to produce. Some of my favorite moments occurred listening to 'Personalities' sing "Take Me Out To The Ball Game" at Wrigley Field, home of the Chicago Cubs. One guest had the words in front of him, but lost his place. One forgot the One, Two, Three strikes you're out phrase and one just stopped singing. A couple of guests appeared to be on adrenalin enhancers. These guests were known by their first names…MIKE (Ditka) and OZZY (Osborne). There were others, but no one gave us more fun than those two!

Apparently they were not afraid!

FIST BUMPS

I have been a soccer referee for 35 years in over 2,000 games as Center & AR (Asst. Referee). Most of my early years were spent with AYSO (American Youth Soccer Organization). I continue to referee with AYSO – a wonderful organization. After a couple of years I included Club Soccer (where you are often alone) and then High Schools.

After each game the teams line up facing each other on the half way line. The intent is to high five or shake the opponents hand in a display of sportsmanship. Wouldn't you know, some players (boys & girls) just can't behave themselves. Number 5 on the green team was jawing at me the entire game.

How about 'gob' of spittle on my hand! Referees watch for this at all times. When the players are finished it is then time to shake the referees hands. Guess what, Number 9 on the white team questioned why he received a caution (Yellow Card) for his dangerous slide tackle. I hold my arm out straight, close my fist and let them figure out what they are suppose to do! A couple of seconds of hesitation usually brings a touch to my hand and a smile like 'this is cool' After an AYSO game this past fall, a young lady commented "He does a 'fist bump' just like President Obama and his wife". Her coach (whom I have known for years) was right behind her and exclaimed "Referee Edmonds has been doing that for years." I smiled and said, "But now I know it has a name!"

PAINTINGS

What picture, photograph or painting has had an impact on your life? 5,000 people will have 5,000 varied memories. Unfortunately many of these memory photos are negative! Many tell of fear filled moments in their youth. Some are gentle, but most are a challenge to the maturation of the person. Sister Sharon (my actual sister as opposed to three aunts who are sisters/nuns) purchased a Keane painting many years ago that hung on the wall at the top of mom & dad's stairs. It was mucho fun to come home after an evening of bar hopping, start up those stairs and watch those two huge sad black eyes follow you to the top.

I'm sure the six of us siblings each in our own way were rude to that painting. I know I often gave a Lilly Tomlin 'Razzberry' and at least one sister or brother must have 'flipped off' the intruder at the top of the stairs at least once! Son Grant, talked about a fear he remembers from his youth. He always dreaded going to Oshkosh during the holidays to visit relatives. He loved being with his cousins and grandma and grandpa, but that painting of the girl with the BIG EYES at the top of the stairs freaked him out. Fortunately he survived, but had he required therapy, because of BIG EYES, I would have insisted any and all Doctor bills be sent directly to sister Sharon.

For many years Margaret Keane was married to a man who claimed credit for what she painted. To prove she was in fact the artist and not her former husband, before a Federal Judge and jury in court she painted an original oil on canvas. When her ex-husband was asked to paint by the judge, his reply was: "I can't today, because I have a sore shoulder." Margaret continues to paint those Big Eyes we have come to love so dearly.

FRIENDS

Television situational comedies often mirror our lives. The show FRIENDS was a huge, long running hit! Six characters were for the most part, never on the 'same page'. They often got close, but had so many relationship fears! SEINFELD's zany quartet presented us with a new set of everyday problem sort of fears! EVERYBODY LOVES RAYMOND treated us with laughs for years. Fears were on constant display every episode, each week, for each show. Humor resolved all the fears while the characters regrouped for next week.

Starting in kindergarten, each year of our lives presents us with different sets of fears mostly resolved with the help of family, teachers and friendly classmates.

JACKIE ROBINSON

Living in a townhouse complex, nine months of the year I'm able to swim in the pool. Recently I shared the pool with 4 high school seniors and one of them mentioned Jackie Robinson. I asked what prompted him to mention Jackie Robinson and he said recently he was part of a conversation questioning what it must have been like for him, to be the first black player in major league baseball. I told them one of the greatest moments of my life was sitting next to Jackie Robinson for 20 minutes in a limo.

Edmonds & Curley and Jackie Robinson, were guests on The Mike Douglas Show in Philadelphia. During his segment on the show he spoke lovingly about his wife Rachel, who was a nurse. In the limo I told Jackie I had a degree in nursing and the conversation was off and running. He asked how Thom (who was up front with the driver making him laugh…) and I formed the Comedy Team. I mentioned that three months of my nurses training took place at Children's Hospital in Milwaukee. There was a female nurses' party and of course I was in attendance. There was this 6' 5" comic telling stories with 'sound effects' that created laughter for most of the night! Seven years later we became EDMONDS & CURLEY.

Jackie asked where I was born and I said Oshkosh and like everyone else he said "Oshkosh B'gosh". I mentioned that years ago, until I arrived at Fort Leonard Wood, Missouri for Army Basic Training, I had never met anyone who was not caucasian. He gave me a wry smile and said, "You and millions more." Jackie unfortunately passed on two years later. Forty years later I refereed an AYSO soccer match adjacent to the famous Rose Bowl in Pasadena and the field I refereed on?

...JACKIE ROBINSON FIELD...

TONIGHT SHOW

In September of 1969 the yearly fears of all Chicago Cubs fans was in full bloom… the Cubbies were tankin! The good news was Lynn & Joey's marriage of two months was working out nicely AND Edmonds & Curley were auditioning for the Tonight Show starring Johnny Carson. The audition took place in New York City at the John Vicar Theater. When we arrived, talent coordinator Shirley Wood said "There's the stage and the microphone, show me your four minutes". "Microphone? There's two of us." Shirley stated that our manager only requested one. FEAR? Yeah!

Somehow we adapted and were told to call Ms. Wood the next day. So the next day I called and Shirley asked if we would be available the second week of October to make our 1st appearance on the Tonight Show. Silence…for a moment I said nothing and then, "We are available!" YIPPEEEE! Our appearance was scheduled for Wednesday and a local clothing store in Oshkosh placed a classy ad in the paper congratulating us. We flew to NYC and prepared for the show. The Doctors routine is what they wanted. Prior to the five pm taping Shirley met us in the green room and the rest was a 'blur' of activity. We waited, and we waited, and finally, "Guys, we're sorry, but we ran out of time. We'll reschedule next week."

The following Wednesday we are again in the green room. The guest host is Carl Reiner. The show moves along nicely and finally…"Guys you're up next." A few minutes later standing behind the curtain we hear Mr. Reiner announce: "Making their first television appearance, from Oshkosh Wisconsin, please welcome Joey & Thom…EDMONDS & CURLEY!" The guy opened the curtain and said "Good Luck." I smiled… Performing this Doctors Routine at 400 high schools in front of thousands of students this past year, I knew exactly what we were going to do! Walking to the floor marks, I recalled telling Thom that "Someday we'll do this routine on the Tonight Show!" We could not have performed better.

The next morning on the plane, we realized the power of the Tonight Show! Dozens of passengers were congratulating us. In 1983 shortly before we made our last TV appearance on 'Evening at the IMPROV' Carl Reiner was in attendance and I went over to him and said, "Mr. Reiner my name is Joey Edmonds and he interrupted, "The Doctors Routine…that was a great routine!" Made my day! Two months later we were again scheduled for another appearance on the Tonight Show and Johnny would be host. That was a wild night before and after the show! Lynn was with Thom and me and Don Rickles was one of the guests.

Lynn was in the green room when Don walked in and spotted her. With her flowing blond pony tail and wonderful laugh, Rickles gravitated to her. Rickles said "And you are with who?" She pointed to me. Rickles said…"You're with HIM?" Huge laugh! I escorted Lynn into the audience telling her I would return after the show. Once again we nailed it! Johnny said good night to America and we settled near the band as the audience departed. In what seemed like a minute or so, the audience was gone and we made our way to the desk to meet Johnny. We thanked him for having us, shook hands and at that moment he froze…staring beyond us into the audience…one lone figure (Lynn) was making her way to the stage… I turned and said…"Oh that's my wife", and Don

Rickles entered and said "Don't worry, she's with me." Johnny was the best ever, but I'll never forget that fearful look.

Very private man…

<u>COPACABANA</u>

MAY 29, 1970 EDMONDS & CURLEY
BEST OF LUCK TO YOU ON YOUR DEBUT AT THE COPACABANA.
WARM REGARDS – JULES PODELL

What a wonderful, warm greeting that telegram was. Warmth quickly turned to FEAR! For 14 days in May and June three shows a night, we were the opening act for the TEMPTATIONS!

Prior to the first show we met JULES PODELL. A rotund sixty something pit bull of a man with a voice of gravel. He loudly gave us succinct instructions: "Your audiences are High School prom kids. You have 15 minutes…no more…no less and keep it clean! Also, stay out of the kitchen…the waiters are in and out…in and out. Now get on stage and be funny!" That voice was so grating! It dawned on me that if he had a wife, she probably left years ago.

The stage was 8 ft wide and 6 ft deep with an 8 piece orchestra behind the stage. We had our 2 microphones on detachable stands. When the TEMPTATIONS sang there was a thick & heavy stand with 5 'arms' with microphones at the ends. SMALL STAGE!

We always started our show with the Jet Plane routine with Pilot Thom & Co-Pilot Joey. Pilot Thom talks to the tower in a 'garbled-graveled' voice for about 15 seconds! It did not last for 15 seconds this show. Jules Podell thought Thom was imitating him and cut the power! The sound technician/M.C. quickly turned it back on. We finished our set to nice applause and left the stage and ran into Jules who was livid.

"Don't you ever again make fun of me…blah, blah, blah"! I was not shy…"Mr. Podell, that voice is part of our Routine! It has nothing to do with you! Please watch and listen during our next show!"

Opening night was very special because 'celebrities' attended in droves to see the TEMPTATIONS. We impressed everybody and cards were being exchanged. Thom & I just went with the flow. We got to know the 'Temps' as we called them, especially MELVIN the bass singer. Each time I saw him I did my best impression of him by lowering my tenor voice and saying "Helooow Melvin" and he would respond at the bottom of his range…" Helooow Joey" I laughed 3 times nightly.

Each show was wilder than the one before! These were High School students smoking and DRINKING! "Clean up at table 21" was a common mantra each show during those 14 nights! The last night the COPA added a fourth show. As usual it was wall to wall. We were delayed while the COPA scurried to find more tables and chairs. We stood off to the side shaking our heads. Even if they located more tables and chairs where would they put them?

Finally the sound technician/M.C. attempted to welcome everyone. The room was so loud and disorganized we realized later that he had introduced EDMONDS & CURLEY three times.

We got to the stage and Thom did some sound effects and the room seemed to settle down. We did our Jet Airplane routine and now we had the audience. We had decided to finish our 43rd show of the engagement with our Cow Milking routine, probably because of the incongruity of it. NYC, COPA, H.S. Prom people, and we were bored doing the same 15 minutes. This routine necessitated Thom using the fingers of his right hand as udders and we were having a ball until I saw a bus boy carrying a small round table inverted on his head and another bus boy carrying two chairs. YEP! They walked to the stage and manuvered the table and 2 chairs between us.

A couple in full prom regalia sat down and we just stood there laughing with the audience. Finally I said, "Have fun in college." And we left.

TRAINS

I have traveled on trains in Chicago, NYC, London, Scotland, Germany, California, AmTrak, etc., etc. Whatever the destination I was always thrilled when the doors opened and I stepped back to earth. Being a life long *Claustrophobic*, trains and I are not ideal companions.

The first time I stepped on the extremely long escalators that transported one deep into the underground 'TUBE' in London, my brain was telling me; "No…No What are you doing?" I lived there for over a year and eventually enjoyed the tube and met many interesting riders. I did learn to travel before or after rush hours and I never sat! Standing at least gave me the option of distancing myself from others (one of a hundred tricks I've learned to minimize *Claustrophobic* "moments").

Years ago one of my sisters traveling from Wisconsin to Texas paid for a sleeper car. When she climbed onto the bed she had a Claustrophobic "moment" and spent the night with her face against the window, watching the moon disappear.

Hartsfield-Jackson International Airport in Atlanta has trains that whisk you from terminal to terminal. At least a half dozen times I have chosen to not board the train because it appeared to be excessively crowded (another of the hundred tricks). I recently watched a TV newscast showing passengers in China trying to board a train. The train was already full, but 4 or 5 of the police interlocked their arms and literally pushed passengers into the train.

It was like the starting gate at a horse race where helpers reach over, grasp wrists and 'load' horses into the gate!

<u>AND THEY'RE OFF!</u>

POLITICIANS

I grew up in the Republican Sate of Wisconsin, home of the Ripon Society located in the city of the same name. I knew none of this until 1964 when as part of THE TRI-ADDS, a folk singing trio, we were sent to Washington D.C. to help promote the election of Barry Goldwater. I had never been to our nation's capitol and knew nothing about politics. I didn't know my dad voted republican until the early 80's when he abandoned the GOP after Reagan came into office. He was livid that we the people vote in politicians, (many of whom receive bribe money from lobbyists) and then they immediately forget why we voted them in.

He often said "This is the greatest country in the world… Never fear anything except politicians!"

SPOONING

Or as I refer to it, *Claustrophobia*!

Newly weds have many adaptations to their lives and mostly these changes are what makes it exciting. Think back to the early days of your marriage (or not). Warm, wonderful, and comfortable memories. Being able to hug and/or kiss whenever the urge presents itself. Now it is time to retire for the night and your partner is in bed facing away from you. You get in bed and snuggle close and hug. CONGRATULATIONS. You are now SPOONING! What could possible be bad about that? Nothing except if you are claustrophobic and you are facing away from your partner and the partner spoons with you. Within seconds you will struggle to be 'free'

...and move to the other bedroom!

BASEBALL

America's past time starts each year in early April and climaxes with the World Series in late October. Each season hundreds of fans have the opportunity to catch a baseball traveling at the speed of light with no glove. More often dozens of fans are simultaneously diving to avoid being hit by the round misscle. Each time a foul ball leaves the bat a comedy moment is created. Living for 26 years in Chicago Lynn and I observed numerous balls hit into the Wrigley Field grand stands.

One day we decided to become bleacher bums and fearlessly sat in the second row in left field on the hardwood bench. What an experience that turned out to be.

By the third inning many of the fans were already on their 2nd or 3rd beer and the language was quite colorful. I wish I could remember the name of #17 from the visiting team who hit a high and deep drive into the second row of the left field bleachers. It is possible I suffered a slight concussion protecting Lynn from the crazed fans diving over and thru us in an effort to retrieve the home run ball and then throw it back to the field. I remember Lynn's pony tail was a mess! So we each had a beer and laughed it off. with comments like "Why did we sit so close?" and other inanities.

I remember standing for the 7th inning stretch and singing 'Take me out to the ball game' with Harry Caray. The fans sharing the bleachers with us are now very drunk. In the top of the 8th inning #17 once again stepped to the plate. I joked that this time Lynn should protect me from the ball and the fans behind us. The 1st pitch and *crack* the ball was again headed toward us. Lynn ended up between the bleacher and the wall in the first row and I remember shouting "GET OFF ME!" I was literally at the bottom of a scrum having a claustrophobic moment. Another home run and again fans were wrestling with each other in an attempt to secure the baseball and then throw it back on the field.

That evening we watched the sports news and there we were…twice. Of course we video taped it and replayed it a few times. We never again returned to the bleachers.

Son Grant graduated from Butler University located in Indianapolis and for three years he was an editor at the FOX-TV affiliate station. One day he came to work and another editor enthusiastically insisted he watch 'this'! A video from the Detroit affiliate was being shown nationwide. A young man is seen exiting a tunnel in the outfield bleachers at Tiger Stadium both hands filled with 'ball park' food and drink. He makes his way to his seat and turns to sit down at the precise moment a line drive home run baseball strikes him in the groin.

Food and drink are everywhere and the reaction of the fan was what you would expect...shock and pain! Grant's fellow editor played it over and over to uncontrollable laughter.
It was during a slow motion playing that Grant exclaimed! " STOP!
back it up...now freeze it...Oh my god! That's JOHN my high school friend "!
And indeed it was John. Grant sent the video to John and commented someday John could show it to his future family.
It has been 12 years ...still no Children.

FROZEN LAKES

Thomas (never Tom) a classmate from high school who I saw recently at our 50th reunion, could not wait to tell me his adventures on Lake Winnebago during the last few winters. I remember saying at least 3 times…"Are you kidding me?"

Lake Winnebago is the largest lake in Wisconsin (20 miles n/s and 10 miles e/w). Oshkosh is on the western shore, Fond du Lac at the south end and the twin cities of Neenah-Menasha to the north. When the lake freezes each winter there are numerous activities that make oh so many Oshkosh natives oh so happy!

I have named these the Thomas Chronicles! Thomas proceeded with Adventure # 1

"Four years ago my wife and I drove our snowmobiles from Oshkosh toward Fond du Lac on the frozen lake.
There is a restaurant about 12 miles south and we traditionally watch the Packer games with two other adventurous couples. We park in a small cove a few hundred yards from the restaurant.

After a few beverages and a Packers victory, we left the restaurant and made our way to our snowmobiles.

<u>Where are the snowmobiles?</u>

"Six of them...... GONE!"

JE: "Are you kidding me?"

Thomas (never Tom) continued..."Three years ago my grandson asked to borrow my NEW snowmobile and I made sure he took the chain link and lock.

Late afternoon and we had not heard from him. Then my cell phone rang and my wonderful grandson informed me the snowmobile was still 'chained' to the dock, but had broken through the ice and was under water!"

(2) JE: "Are you kidding me?"

Thomas (never Tom) continued…"Two years ago in early February, the winds of Lake Winnebago caused the lake to break from the shoreline and 100 plus cars were on their own pizza pan floating on the lake. National newscasts showed the cars on the island of ice with no place to go. Guess whose four door bright red truck was parked in the middle of the island?

It took four days but not one vehicle was lost."

3)JE: " Are you kidding me?"

"One year ago…………….We spent the winter in Florida."

(4) JE "Good job Tom!"

FAILURE

Prior to each of my FUN~Seminars, I pass out post-it notes and ask the participants to jot down their 1st, 2nd, & 3rd fear… #1 being the worst fear. FAILURE is always one of the three. It is fun and informative listening to their stories and group discussions.

JOHN DOE

****

Growing up in a household of lawyers Mom, Dad, Grandpa and soon-to-be-lawyer-older sister, I was rarely included during the nightly extended cocktail hour prior to our 7 or 8 PM dinner. Oh, I was there, but family chats were always about 'the job'! We had money so I never wanted for things, but money was constantly a reference point. Mostly it was dad reminding me that I would be the 3rd generation lawyer in the family.

**I knew before entering college I was not going to follow grandpa nor dad nor sister nor mom into the field of law!
I decided to pursue a course in Pediatric Medicine.**

Mom and sis were fine, but the men folk were pissed. "How could I not continue what they started?" (I took a chance…) "Grandpa, Dad, you talk about what you started…Started what? …How come you never had your own firm?" (The longest silence ever!) "We'll continue this some other time son. You want to study medicine? Study hard because second chances are rare! Good luck! " I'm now a junior and doing well, but that possibility of failure is always with me! That's my life…you are welcome to it!

JANE DOE

****

When I was five I was introduced to Soccer. I am an only child and it was special for me to play a game with other girls and boys my age. My parents were always 'there for me'. We were a happy family. Once I entered the U12 Division Soccer things changed at home. I didn't know exactly what was happening, but I knew mom would get upset at dad and I didn't know why. Two weeks later during our game, dad was told to leave the field.

I was clueless but continued on. After the game dad picked me up and gave me a big hug. He said he was sorry and that it would not happen again. Now I really was clueless. Mom suggested dad tell me why he left the field. All I remember is dad was told to leave the field because he was causing a disturbance. A disturbance? I looked to mom for help. She explained that dad was shouting and arguing with the referee and finally told to leave the game. Dad continued to watch most of my games…always from a distance. As I got older I also played girls basketball and again dad watched from a distance. Basketball was fun, but I loved soccer! Running all the time and making goals…lots of goals!

In High School I was moved up to the varsity soccer team. Dad for the most part kept silent during the games. But slowly I noticed a change in him. During my junior year I was starting to attract attention from colleges. At the end of my junior season we had a serious family 'talk'. All of a sudden much of the fun was being removed from the game. We decided one by one to talk about any subject. The conversation moved immediately to soccer. What an event that turned out to be.

"Dad, you have always been a wonderful father…what happens to you during my sporting events?"

Long pause…..

"When I was six I started playing T-ball and fell in love with baseball. I was a top ranked player in High School and drafted by the Cardinals. I was invited to spring training and did well, but my temper always seemed to get me in trouble. I was sent to class A and hit over 300. The last game of the season I led off with a double. I then stole 3rd and on the catcher's errant throw headed for home. The last thing I remember was crashing into the catcher. I woke up in the ambulance on the way to the hospital with my left leg in a brace. My knee required major surgery and my baseball dreams were finished.

For years, with your mom's help, I put all of that behind. Then you started athletics and my competitive nature returned." Fast forward... I did receive a soccer scholarship and my dad was thrilled. Being 3 hours away, they were able to see all of my home games. Dad was already talking about the Olympics two years in the future! Pressure not to fail was getting intensified. The final home game of the season I blew out my knee.

Bye Bye Soccer! (yeah)

FUTURE

FEARFUL:

FEAR will become a mantra. Each day, time will be spent obsessed with who, what, where?

OR

OPTOMISTIC:

Do not be afraid to DREAM!
Create a DREAM.
Live your DREAM.

Special Thanks: Editors

Actress & Sister-in-law Judith Drake.

Brother-in-law & fellow Gemini,
POET – Dale J. Bilek

Son Grant Edmonds ~ Author:
LoveG.E.A.R.S.
A RELATIONSHIP TOOL BOOK
@ Amazon.Com

Daughter Kate who has more fun than her dad! (and that's a lot)

Ray Juliano
(Thank You)

HELP

Here are sources to visit for additional materials.

I highly recommend

E F T

Emotional Freedom Techniques

www.emofree.com

The Internet has everything!

My best to you, Joey

www.ingramcontent.com/pod-product-compliance
Lightning Source LLC
Chambersburg PA
CBHW061034050726
47592CB00004B/1432
9780578037011